OCTOPUS

Harper & Row, Publishers
New York, Evanston, San Francisco, London

OCTOPUS

by Evelyn Shaw
Pictures by Ralph Carpentier

A Science I CAN READ Book

Trade Standard Book Number 06-025558-7
Harpercrest Standard Book Number 06-025559-5

Library of Congress Catalog Card Number: 74-135779

To Susan, Jason,
Russell
(*and* Max)

OCTOPUS

An eye looks out of a hole

in the rocks in the sea.

The eye watches

small fishes swimming by.

9

The eye belongs to an octopus.

The body of the octopus
is fat and round like a balloon.

She has eight long arms.

They are wrapped around her body.

The octopus is ready
to leave her home
to look for food.

Just then there is a crash.

A small boat

bumps into the rocks.

The boat backs up

and chugs away.

The rocks fall down

to the bottom of the sea.

Little fishes swim wildly

in the water.

A crab digs into the soft sand.

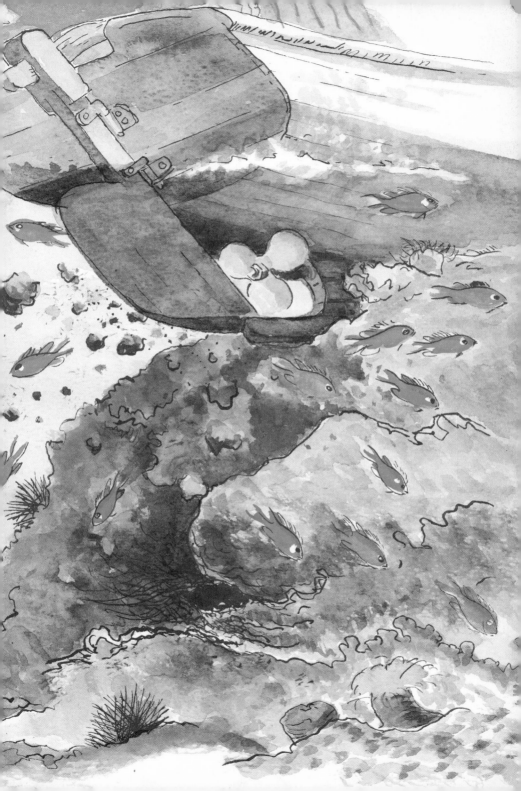

The octopus turns pale with fear.

She huffs and puffs.

Her body grows smaller,

then bigger,

then smaller again.

Suddenly a big rock falls

in front of her home.

The octopus is trapped inside.

She tries to push the rock away,

but it is too heavy.

With the tip of an arm

she finds a little opening.

She makes her body

small and flat.

This is easy to do

because an octopus has no bones.

She squeezes out.

Then her body becomes round again.

The octopus stands up

on her eight arms

and walks away.

At that moment another big rock
falls down.
Now the octopus can never
get into her home again.

The octopus is in danger.

She needs a new home.

She needs a place

where she can hide

and rest and eat.

She starts to hunt for one.

The octopus slides

over some rocks.

She finds a hole.

She puts the tip of an arm

into the hole

to see if it is empty.

But it is the home of a little fish.

The fish swims out

and bites the octopus.

The octopus goes on.

The next hole she finds

belongs to another octopus.

He comes out to defend his home.

They start to fight.

They twist their arms

around each other.

They change color from light to dark

and then back to light.

They slide over the rocks.

Finally she pulls away.

He goes back into his home.

She is not hurt,

but she has not found

a place to live.

The octopus walks on her eight arms
to a bed of seaweed.
She stops there to rest.
Her body turns brown.
Her skin becomes
rough and bumpy.
It is hard for other animals
to see her.
She looks just like the seaweed.

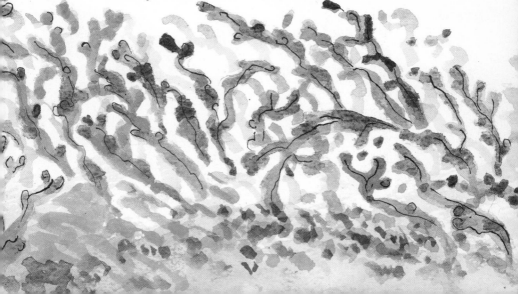

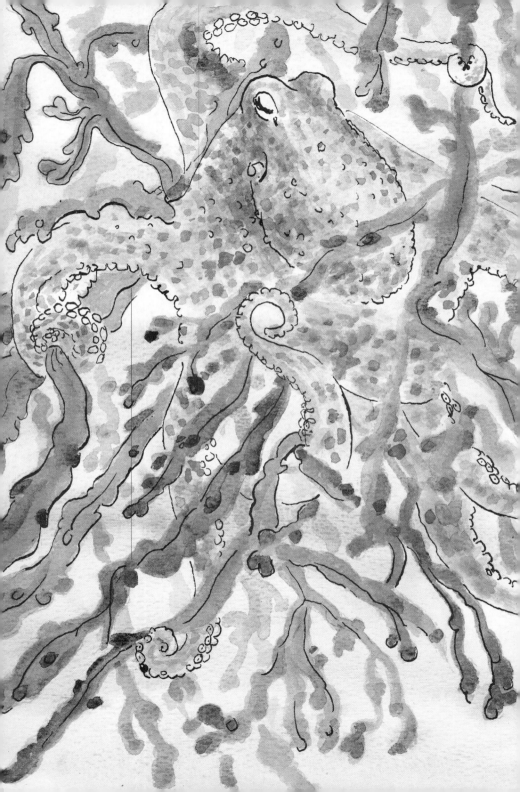

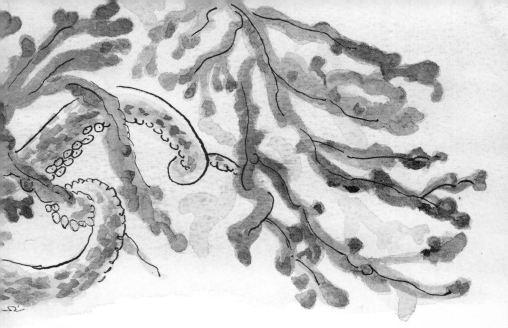

There are other plants in the sea,

but the octopus cannot look like

all of them.

She has only a few colors

in her skin.

She can become

orange-red or brown.

She can become dark or light.

Later on, the octopus leaves

the bed of seaweed.

She touches everything

with the suckers on her arms.

She feels and tastes

with these suckers.

The octopus finds a small shell.

She bites into it

with her strong beak.

After she bites it,

the animal in the shell

cannot move.

She begins to eat the animal.

But the octopus is not safe here.

A moray eel pokes its head

out of a hole.

The eel smells the octopus

and swims toward her.

It wants to eat her.
Suddenly the octopus
sees the eel.

She drops her food.

Her body becomes dark.

She shoots

a cloud of black ink

out of her body.

The ink makes the water dark.

The eel swims into the ink.

It cannot see her.

The octopus gets away.

34

She shoots

jets of water

out of her body.

She moves quickly

through the sea.

When the octopus is safe

she slows down.

She opens her arms

like a parachute.

She glides down to some rocks.

There in the rocks

she finds a hole.

She puts three arms

into the hole.

It is empty.

She goes inside the hole.

She touches every part of it.

It is the right size.

She has found a new home.

The octopus rests there,

watching the sea.

A crab walks toward the rocks.

It is walking sideways.

The octopus watches the crab.

The crab finds a dead fish

and begins to eat it.

The octopus comes out of her home.

She pounces on the crab.

Her body becomes dark.

Her arms spread out

like an open umbrella.

The suckers on her arms

hold the crab tight.

She bites the crab.

It is not able to move.

The octopus drags

the crab into her home.

She cracks the shell

of the crab with her beak.

Then she sucks out the meat.

After she has finished,
she pushes the pieces
of shell outside.

The octopus mated
with a male octopus
several months ago.
Now it is spring.

It is almost time for the octopus
to lay her eggs.
She begins to get ready.
The octopus puts two arms
outside her home.
She finds some small stones.
The octopus holds the stones
with the suckers on her arms.
She pulls the stones into her home.
She places them around the opening.
She makes the opening small.
Big animals cannot get in.

Then she lays her eggs.
She lays hundreds of them
in long thin egg cases.
The octopus puts the egg cases
on rocks inside her home.
She no longer goes out
to look for food.

She guards her eggs.

She keeps little fishes

and shrimps from eating them.

She rubs her arms over the eggs
to keep them clean.
For weeks she does not leave
her home.

At last the eggs hatch.

The octopus has

hundreds of babies.

The babies have

yellow and red dots all over them.

They look like tiny clowns.

They are no bigger than fleas.

They do not have long arms.

They cannot swim very well.

But it is time for them

to leave home.

Their mother stays behind.

She is very thin

because she has not eaten.

She will not live much longer.

The babies go out into the sea.

They float in the water

for about two months.

The little octopuses eat
tiny sea animals.
Some of the little octopuses
are eaten by fishes.
The ones that are left
grow bigger.

Their arms grow long.

They can walk or glide

on their arms.

They can swim well.

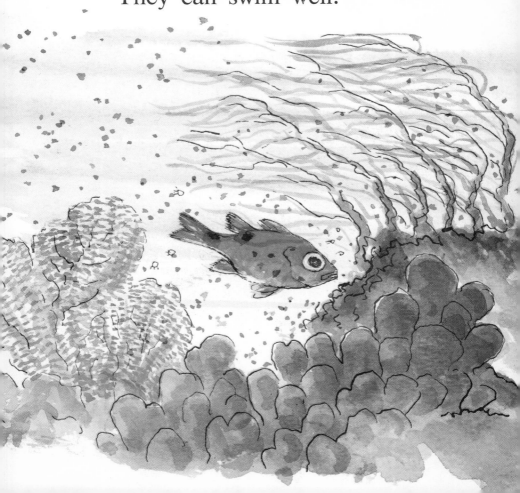

The young octopuses are ready

to start looking

for crabs to eat.

They can touch and taste

with the suckers on their arms.

They can hide

by becoming the color

of rocks and weeds.

They can get away from enemies

by shooting out

dark clouds of ink.

They are ready to find homes.

Two of the young octopuses

come to some rocks.

They move their arms

over the rocks.

Each finds its own hole in the rocks.

60

Each has found a place

where it can hide

and rest and eat.

They have found homes in the sea.

ABOUT THE AUTHOR

Dr. Evelyn Shaw is a curator in the Department of Animal Behavior at The American Museum of Natural History in New York City. Dr. Shaw has studied the behavior of fish for sixteen years. She has watched many kinds of octopuses in the Caribbean and in the Mediterranean.

The octopus in this book is *Octopus vulgaris*, a species which is found in the Mediterranean and Caribbean Seas.